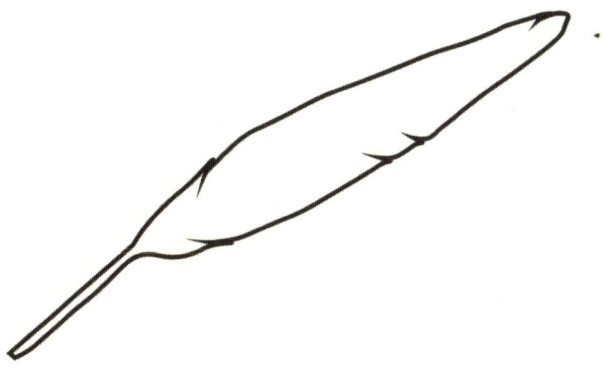

ONCE UPON WING LAKE

Andrea Scarpino

Hoot n Waddle
Phoenix, AZ

Origianlly published in 2017 by Four Chambers Press.
Republished in 2018 by Hoot n Waddle.

Typeset in LTC Goudy Oldstyle
Printed in the United States of America by Biltmore Pro Print

Edited by Jared Duran
Author Photo by Mike Naddeo
Cover & Book Design by Janell Hughes

ISBN 978-1-7323361-2-4
Library of Congress Control Number

10 9 8 7 6 5 4 3 2 1

Published by Hoot n Waddle
Phoenix, AZ

hootnwaddle.com

For Chandler

Then there are some siblings abandoned in the desolate forest.
The wind terrifies them, and they are afraid of the wild animals;
yet, they faithfully support each other.
The little brother knows how to find his way back home.

—Jacob and Wilhelm Grimm

ittle Brother,

You will hear the bear before she appears,
sway-step through early snow.
You will stand quietly, palms at your hips,
wait for her mouth, her teeth on your neck
guiding you past the blueberry field,
deer spring, swallowed whole by trees.
Where Mother can't follow you.
A bear with heavy hips, fur that smells
of blood, burnt coffee, fish.
You won't be strong enough without
her teeth on your neck, each vertebra,
crush of bone. Or the wolf, beleaguered foe,
maybe you wait for the wolf to appear.
How long must you walk these forest trails
before you crouch low, your eyes turned wild,
your hair? How long till the one
who birthed you forgets your face?
Escape, your heart beats.
Scuttle of squirrel, long step of deer.
Branches spring back in release.
Escape. You walk and wait and listen.
Where are the frightening beasts?

ummers on the lake, we climbed the fruit trees,
filled pail after pail with cherries, pears, apples

we sliced into pie. We swam the lagoon,
thick muck of rotting leaves. Late afternoon, sirens:

sky gone orange, strange, green haze of rain, lightning.
Father tuned his radio. Mother stood at the kitchen sink,

blue housedress, bare feet, washed plates from lunch.
We stood at the top of the stairs, *Please come*

to the basement. Our pillows pressed to our chests.
She shook her head, waited to smell sulfur:

Every disaster has its scent—
Or the evening on the back deck: one by one,

the kitchen chairs, her hands, a splintering—
Or the telephone she tore from the wall.

Or the birthday cake she threw at my face.
Or the weeks I refused to speak to anyone but you,

mouth pressed to your ear. The babysitter arrived
with black metal shears in her shirt pocket.

If you're not going to use your tongue,
might as well cut it out. One hand under my chin.

Hello, I said. One word to save myself.
And Father with his glue, pin nails, black paint—

Those were my mother's chairs—
Little Brother: *What do you know for sure?*

To move forward, they say, make peace with the past.
Mother in bed all afternoon, nest of blankets, heating pad.

Scotch in a juice glass. I nestled under her wing,
a baby bird, and she pinched between her fingertips

one long, thin worm. Blue in my feathers, blue in her eyes.
Or the robin's egg we saved in a bowl. Or the swans

we sculpted from clay, blue veins of Mother's hands
as they shaped our necks and beaks. Clay dried to milky rain.

Or the winter we fed a stray cat that froze, one night,
to the front steps, its eyes open. *Save what you can save,*

Mother said, sewed earrings in the hem of a dress,
gold chain in a pocket lining. I craved carrots, oranges,

sand in my bathing suit. I chewed my nails until they bled.
Or the August birds fell from the sky, shattered

their skulls on the deck. We buried a gull's curved beak,
hummingbird's emerald throat, thin feet. *Mother Nature*

isn't kind, Mother said. She stripped your clothes,
ran water ice-cold, filled the yellow mixing bowl.

Lifted the bowl over your head. Held it there like the sun.
Then poured. Your skin raised red across your chest,

shoulders, little-boy wings. I stood in the empty doorway.
Or the night Mother followed me, stagger-step,

with a kitchen knife in her hands. I ran to my bedroom,
turned the lock, jumped from the open window.

And as I fell, wings sprouted from my shoulder blades,
blue in my feathers, blue in her eyes. And I caught myself,

caught wing to blue air, flew fast across the lake's dirt roads
as she beat down my bedroom door.

nce upon a time there was a sparrow
swallowed by a man who wanted him dead.
But the sparrow continued to sing
inside his captor's throat. So the man
gave his wife an axe and told her to kill
the bird. Then opened his mouth.
Mother opened her mouth and I flew in,
preened my feathers to blue, catch and sheen
of watertight, of iridescence. I sang,
mouth open wide. And Mother held a knife
to her throat, my throat. And so I learned
the gravity of her round body, pull of flight.
I learned how blade fractures blue sky.

other's voice on the phone:

Why are you so afraid? Dinner a couple of nights a week
at your house, Thanksgiving, Christmas.

What are you so afraid will happen if you spend time with me?
Like I'm some kind of wicked witch—

Once upon a time Mother rose from the sea,
kelp-tangled, salt-streaked,
cleaved open her hands like shells.
Little birds, she sang, *Come to me.*
And we did, perched on her shoulders,
opened our beaks to drink.
In our throats, a salty sting,
thrashing waves. And she held us there,
net of the tides thrown over our wings,
net of her blue eyes. *Come to me.*
And we beat ourselves against her shoreline.

Once upon a time Mother and Father,
two children, a lake, mute swans.
Once upon a time mute swans and their
cygnets, robins with blue-egged nests,
smell of rotting leaves. And bandits,
a man in brown overalls. Once upon a time
light through apple leaves, and pear,
cherry. We climbed their branches,
called to each other, tree to tree.
And Brother, your golden wings
grew strong in the sun, your shoulders
grew muscled and wide. Golden boy.
Once upon a time we knew bird-flight:
wind's lift and soar, dip and delay,
long glide, pivot and dive, knew
how to ride a current, sun to our backs,
and then, downdraft, a plummet
we knew how to right.

ittle Brother: *What do you know for sure?*

We were children once, remember?
We knotted twine, hid bread in our pockets,

sifted gold nuggets through metal sieves.
We gathered candles and long matches,

tracked beasts, drew maps of secret caves.
We slipped down the stairs on our stomachs,

wrote notes with lemon juice on paper we stained
with Mother's tea. Our hearts beat too loudly

for us to sleep. And we lived in a place
called Wing Lake: mallard ducks, geese,

blue heron that reigned on one leg.
Blue in my feathers, blue in your eyes.

Spring, we caught minnows by the bucket,
tadpoles that died before they grew legs.

We watched the sky for the swans' return,
worn feathers, travel-thin necks. They told us

the secret of flight, wind gathered in shoulder blades,
how turtles snap from below, how quickly

a mother turns. We built a hideout from cattails
and fallen branches, swept the dirt floor,

made weapons from stone to battle bandits.
At night, so many stars, milky line of the galaxy,

so many lightning bugs we caught in jars.
Fall came with its rotting leaves, blue of the sky

turned steel, glint of an axe and the blood it finds.
The lake turned itself to ice. We read stories

of Arctic adventurers, planned our own escape:
what clothing we'd need, how many strong men,

ice picks, deer to keep us from starving.
We packed soup, instant oatmeal, sardines.

We must be ready, always, to run—
I was snow covering our tracks,

you were wind sweeping away our scent.
I was the core we cut in lake ice.

You the hook of our dropped line.

We were children once.
Light shone in the trees. Rocks breathed,

watched over us. The mute swans nested,
a jumble of twigs and lake grass

we watched until two cygnets emerged.
A third, the weakest, lay on its side in mud.

Its open beak, fluttering breath.
We dripped water from our fingertips, fed it

what worms we could find, covered it with felt,
drew it a picture of the lake.

It died one morning before we arrived.
Mother Swan had to think of her other babies,

Mother said. The other two grew strong,
waited each afternoon for bread.

Summer grew sticky with thunderstorms,
sirens. Cattails rattled a warning song—

Every disaster has its scent.
One evening, the mother turned,

grabbed a cygnet by its thin neck
and held it below the water,

small beating wings against wide chest.
We threw rocks, screamed,

you waved a long stick over your head.
When the mother let go, the cygnet bled,

red open wound we could see from shore.
We begged Mother to call a vet.

Mother Nature isn't kind, she said.
Feathers covered in blood.

And so we learned what hurt parents hold.
We learned only one of us could survive.

nce upon a time you fell from the sky,
Brother,
blue of your feathers, blue of your eyes,
Brother,
and a neighbor came to watch me,
Brother,
cooked oatmeal with syrup, honey,
Brother,
as if to fill my teeth with cavities,
Brother,
as if to fatten me, my mouth,
Brother,
blistered with sweet, but you arrived,
Brother,
spread your thin wings above lake ice,
Brother,
I longed for you, I dreamed you into life,
Brother,
and then it was you and I.

nce upon a time there was a boy
who slept while his mother sewed,
her hands smoothing fabric, knotting thread,
her foot rocking pedal to wooden floor.
He woke to a stack of mended clothes,
his mother asleep in her chair.
And he grew tall and broad. She grew
a crooked back. Years passed.
You and I held hands as we lay
in our bunk beds, listened to the start
and stop of a sewing machine, hum
in our chests, hum in the plaster walls.
The nights were long for all of us,
those living, those dead. Some mornings
when dawn opened over the lake, we wept.

ittle Brother: *What do you know for sure?*

We picked apples I cooked into sauce,
sour cherries I baked into pie. Long afternoons,

I turned down pages in Mother's cookbooks,
found recipes to cure our family's aches:

ginger preserved in thick syrup, pistachio rice,
vegetable soup with kidney beans. O of Mother's face.

O of measuring cups and tablespoons.
The week I turned thirteen, cake mix sat boxed

on the countertop until I baked it,
stirred powdered sugar and butter frosting,

lit candles I blew out with one breath—

other hid a pistol, wore Swedish clogs.

You held my hand from the bunk below.

We caught snakes in Father's socks.

The dog caught a goose, broke its neck in his teeth.

Mother drew swans with heart faces,
a cape of willow leaves around the cygnets.

Ice clinked against her wedding band.

Her broken finger healed with a bend—

One afternoon, sky between rain and snow,
I fell through lake ice. My knit hat

covered my eyes, water filled my snowsuit.
And I thought, *Just go slow*, stroke by stroke

like my swim instructor taught. And I thought, *Survive*.
Stroke by stroke to the edge of the lake where Father

grabbed my hood, pulled me from icy mud.
Mother furious. And I so proud I saved myself—

other married three times, divorced.
Mother married four times.

Mother married three or four or five—
Mother said Father abandoned us.

Father said Mother packed while he slept,
called a friend to drive us away.

I refused to speak to anyone but you.
I refused to eat anything but chocolate

in silver wrappers her friend pressed to my hands.
Father hired detectives, filed emergency orders,

recorded our conversations on small cassettes.
The judge in his quiet chambers, short hair

and wool pants, clipboard filled with questions.
I refused to speak to anyone but you.

You refused to leave the car. I sat in the back,
held your hand across the seat.

Mother called men *husband, dear friend,*
my better half, best chum, man of my dreams.

Her friend kept bowls of chocolate on her desk,
bookshelves, bedroom dresser, kitchen sill.

I unwrapped them one by one, held their silver to light—

ittle Brother: *The men*

Mother called husband or the men she married?
The men with whom she lived? The men whose last names

she took? And who brought her to California?
Was that before or after Marblehead?

ittle Brother: *Does anyone have a good childhood?*

Once upon a time Mother took long drives
with a family friend Sunday afternoons.
He was older than her parents,
wore sharp hats and leather gloves.
She was a pretty girl, broad face,
loose curls she swept across her forehead.
Grandmother bought her a special coat
for her weekend drives, special ribbons
for her hair. Maybe, sometimes, the friend
stopped the car by the side of the road.
Maybe the radio played.
Maybe they rolled down the windows,
watched for deer, long shadow of a hawk.
Maybe he touched the bow in her hair.
Maybe she laughed quickly,
wished her palms opened to flight.

nce upon a time Mother watched
wrestling on the black and white TV
her father built. First in the neighborhood.
She loved how the grainy bodies moved,
all muscle, action, slick with Vaseline.
So different from the men she knew
in neatly pressed pants, quick to silence,
disappear into another room.
She begged to invite her friends,
serve juice from the glass punchbowl.
They took off their shoes and jumped
on the couch, screamed for their favorites,
pulled each other's ribboned hair.
They beat their fists to their chests.

ittle Brother: *What do you know for sure?*

was always afraid.

andits?

Bandits were the least of it:
a man in brown overalls,

neighbors robbed at gunpoint.
Our brush with death, Mother called it.

I woke in the night to check the front door,
search for the pistol Mother hid.

I tucked a knife under my bed.
Or the sky gone orange, strange,

scent of rotting eggs, of lake muck
stirred with the row boat's oars.

Trees bent low in the wind. Sirens.
Or Mother's age and murmuring heart:

nine months of dizziness, vomiting,
beer after beer to calm her stomach.

She hired a housekeeper who cleaned the toilet,
washed the floors on hands and knees.

The woman knelt, scrubbing,
a bright blue sponge in her hands.

Mother held me to her heavy waist.
Then stepped, one foot on the woman's hand.

Balanced. Took a second step. Stood there.
Bare feet on bare hands.

Sunlight came through the windows,
fall in its bright decay. Father appeared,

said Mother's name, one short, sharp syllable.
And Mother stepped away.

The woman's hands turned red.
I watched her stare at them, say nothing.

nce upon a time Mother's gravity
spun us quickly, moons broken
from her rock and dust, carbon and rage.
Each with our own rotation, orbit.
When sun shone, we warmed our hands
to her face. When shadow in our bones—
And Father a distant planet, solar system
we knew we couldn't reach.

ittle Brother: *It wasn't your job to protect me.*

Once upon a time your bones
as fine as robin wings,
as summer light, golden boy,
blue of your feathers—
Staph spread knees to chest.
Your skin blackened in bands.
Your body splayed, naked,
IVs in your hands, neck,
tangle of cords, machinery.
Your body strapped
to a board. I held your feet,
toes, the only skin
not needle-pricked, septic.
O of my face   your face—

other's voice on the phone:

Is this my little bird? My little blue-eyed bird
fallen from her robin's nest? Little bird flown away—

Don't forget your Mother is your best friend—

always say my daughter isn't kind—

 always say, Don't ever have children. They ruin your life—

ear Daughter I held as your skin
blushed bright,

before you called my name, you suckled ice.
Before you held my hand, you fisted snow.

The nurse said a child born in winter light
will always turn from her mother.

Before you crawled, you pushed yourself
from my lap, my arms.

Your heart must be made of coal.
Or else your chest is empty space.

Dear Daughter, you failed to love me first.

ear Golden Boy,

Boy I Carried Through So Much Sickness.
Boy Who Almost Died.
Boy Who Took His Sister's Hand Instead of Mine.
Boy Who Followed His Sister into the Woods.
Boy Grown Shoulder-Wide, Soaring Height.
Boy Grown Flight—

I long and long and long.

ittle Brother: *What do you know for sure?*

nce upon a time we were Dorothy
and Scarecrow on our summer camp's
outdoor stage when the sky darkened,
sirens filled the trees. Playbills and
paper cups caught the wind. Lightning.
Every disaster has its scent—
Mother and Father sat in their seats.
The Tin Man finally took up his line
shouting Dorothy's safe return.
And so we learned the show must go on.
We'd have to pull ourselves from the stage.

My legs loose in my hip sockets
flailed under me, bones in my back creaked,

each muscle pulled, each vertebra, rib.
I held my hand to the wall, steadied

my shifting head on my neck. Kids jostled past.
I could not speak to them, throat bitten

by bands of cold. Fever broke across my chest,
deep in my ears ached. The sofa's white cushions—

how did I get home?— pushed against
my shoulder blades, Mother's fur coat

heavy across my legs. And I became the beasts
I knew the coat contained, brown bear

stalking salmon, rumble low in my throat;
wild eyes of the mink; grassland foxes;

beaver, wood I spit out in heaps; restless rabbit.
And their skin weighted me to Earth.

Two days, three nights I slept.
And when I stood again, I knew the lives

of the beasts, knew I was one of them,
claw and fur and voice, rip of flesh and bone,

heart beating warm between my teeth.

We fed the mute swans long afternoons,
bread we tore to pieces, rotting apples, pears.

Their necks reached long tracking summer storms.
And we tried to guess their human forms:

once a wicked queen, a king too quiet, too long,
a restless daughter, son who couldn't follow orders.

We knew they blistered in their swan skins
and tried to change them back, *abracadabra*,

breath blown on their wings, white feathers
we held to a burning match. And once,

the cygnets pulled themselves from the lake,
walked across our backyard, pecked at the door

until we opened it. They stood on our kitchen tile,
hissed secrets to our ears: *You must be ready, always,*

to run— how quickly a mother turns—

nce we drove all night to meet Father
in a neighboring state. We shared a plate of eggs

in the hotel diner, played the lobby's arcade games.
Then Father lifted his suitcase to the trunk, drove away.

And once I baked lemon meringue, O of Mother's face
as I served each slice on our holiday plates. And once

we kept lop-eared rabbits, goslings we let swim in the tub,
box turtles, goldfish. And once a man came to the door

in brown overalls, said he needed to read a meter
in our basement. The dog lunged, barking, choking,

mouth foaming white. Mother said no, *sorry*,
closed and locked the door. That night, a man

in brown overalls walked into a neighbor's party,
gunpoint. *Our brush with death,* Mother called it.

And once I lay on the floor of her room as she groaned
through the night. And once I found her at the sink,

blue housedress, bare feet, eating peanut butter from the jar
with a wooden spoon. Suck and swallow of her tongue.

I watched from the doorway as she swayed, one hip
to the countertop, and something rose in my stomach,

beat against my ribs. Breath caught in my throat.
The kitchen blurred, my fingernails began to blue.

What to call it? We were children, once, and the trees
leaned secrets to our ears: *beware— be wary of—*

Ice clinked in Mother's glass. You appeared
in the doorway's darkness and took my hand.

Breathe deep, you said, again and again. I followed
your slow inhale. *We must be ready, always, to run—*

And once I stopped eating, took Mother's sleeping pills,
pain killers, caffeine. I wanted to be so small

I could slip through a window seam, door crack, vent,
I wanted to silence my heavy step. My knees

scraped each other raw, bruises spread down my calves.
I tiptoed, leapt as high as I could. And still, I fell to Earth,

a clamoring. And still, Mother found me. Shadow.
That's what I longed to be. Shadow rising like steam.

nd Little Brother, what do you remember?

Mother left us home alone
three days at a time,
four days.
We ate frozen dinners,
did laundry, fed the dog,
put ourselves to bed,
walked ourselves to the bus.
Sundays
we were never alone,
church after church.
She said Father abandoned us.
She said you had cancer—
that scared me the most.
She said we'd run off to Uruguay.
I remember psychologists.
I remember the judge's chambers.
I remember her hairbrush,
a paddle for spanking—
I couldn't sit down for a week.
I'm sure we both remember the lies—
some you believed—
some you probably still believe.
She called and called the police,
said I was schizophrenic,
said Father stole her checks,
sexual abuse,
got him arrested.
She deserves to die alone.
Not as punishment.
As what she's earned.

nce upon a time whiteout of snow
as we walked home from school.
Don't lose me—   I won't—
whiteout of memories: your naked body,
cold water poured over your head,
black-handled kitchen knives, juice glass
of alcohol, prescription pills, telephone torn
from the wall. Snow in our ears,
against our bare wrists. And we knew
we would die—we'd read stories like this—
and we knew to survive we'd have to turn
our hands into wings, blue of our feathers
glinting. We rose clumsily, rose and dove
through the terrible snow—*Don't lose me—*
I won't— until we could almost see
where the storm met the blue of the sky.

nce I returned to the house.
Tarps hung from the wooden beams,

paint cans stacked in the dining room.
A man in brown overalls sanded the floor.

Vomit was caked to the sink, he said,
dog shit ground in the carpet, broken bottles

of alcohol. We had to return to the studs.
No one decent lived here. O of my face.

And once I stopped answering
Mother's calls. Two weeks. Two months.

I woke in the night with a sticky chest,
milky pus from my breasts.

I woke in the night to her voice:
This is what you get—

Child of my body—

essage left on my phone:

*Your mother has purchased a number of your books
and wants to distribute them to many people.*

*She also wants to regain a relationship with you.
Do you have anything you wish to say to her?*

We sat at my kitchen table,
Brother,
and you said, *She left us alone,*
Brother,
days at a time,
Brother,
she made you stand naked,
Brother,
held a knife, I jumped,
Brother,
you said, *So many lies,*
Brother,
Does anyone have a good childhood?
Brother,
we were drunk,
Brother,
and you reached across the table,
Brother,
held my hand in your own.

pell for a Canvas Bag, Packed.
Spell for a Pouch of Magic Beans.
Spell for Full Moon, for Light in the Trees.
Spell for Wildfire Burning our Tracks.
Spell for Raspberries Ripe on a Bush.
Spell for Thorn-Prick, Rustle of Leaves.
Spell for Yellow Eyes, Glowing.
Spell for Tree-Sharpened Claws.
Spell for Neighbors Who Open Their Doors.
Spell for Porridge, a Glass of Brandy.
Spell for Never Turning Back.

Once upon a time I lay awake in the night,
scent of roasting coffee, baking bread,

sound of the plow clearing snow drifts,
shovel scrape and pile. Winter a glass cage.

Mother's voice in messages left
from her hospital bed:

The doctors found my heart, finally.
Most are on the left but mine is on the right—

Like I'm some kind of wicked witch—
Mother a glass cage. Mirror Mirror:

clink of ice, prescription pills.
Long reach of the lake summer afternoons.

Sirens: *Save what you can save.*
Our wings stretched blue and strong,

wind caught in our shoulder blades.
Once upon a time I lay awake in the night

with falling snow, Mother's messages.
My cuticles bled, hips ached. I craved

tangerine, kumquat, sweet orange bursts
between my teeth. When I slept,

I woke to my hands in pantomime:
lemons seeded for drinks, pith peeled.

The house with its stone and freezing
hallways, overgrown moat, drawbridge

stuck in place. I wore a nightgown
and Mother's fur coat, its lick at my throat,

searched for a hidden staircase,
a bookcase that turned into spring.

When I slept, I dreamed the cygnets grown,
broken through a snow-filled haze,

landed on my front steps.
One with a scar down its neck,

the other broad-shouldered, strong.
Blue of their eyes, blue of winter light.

I dreamed we slid our arms around their wings
and flew away.

cknowledgements

Many thanks to the editors of *Red Wheelbarrow* and *Nine Mile* who published excerpts of this book, often in very different forms.

I am incredibly grateful to Carrie Shipers, Saara Myrene Raappana, Jeff Hoffman, and Lois Melina for reading drafts of this book and providing invaluable feedback. I am also grateful to Chandler Prince for reading my words, sharing his memories, and giving me the okay to publish.

And thanks to Lawrence Karn, who told me the story of his father asking, "What do you know for sure?" and unintentionally began this project.

And as always, thank you to Zac.

bout the Author

Andrea Scarpino is the author of the poetry collections *Once Upon Wing Lake* (Four Chambers Press, 2017), *What the Willow Said as it Fell* (Red Hen Press, 2016) and *Once, Then* (Red Hen Press, 2014). She received a PhD in Creative Writing from Bath Spa University, and an MFA from The Ohio State University. She has published in numerous journals including *The Cincinnati Review*, *Los Angeles Review*, and *Prairie Schooner*, and she served as Poet Laureate of Michigan's Upper Peninsula 2015-2017.